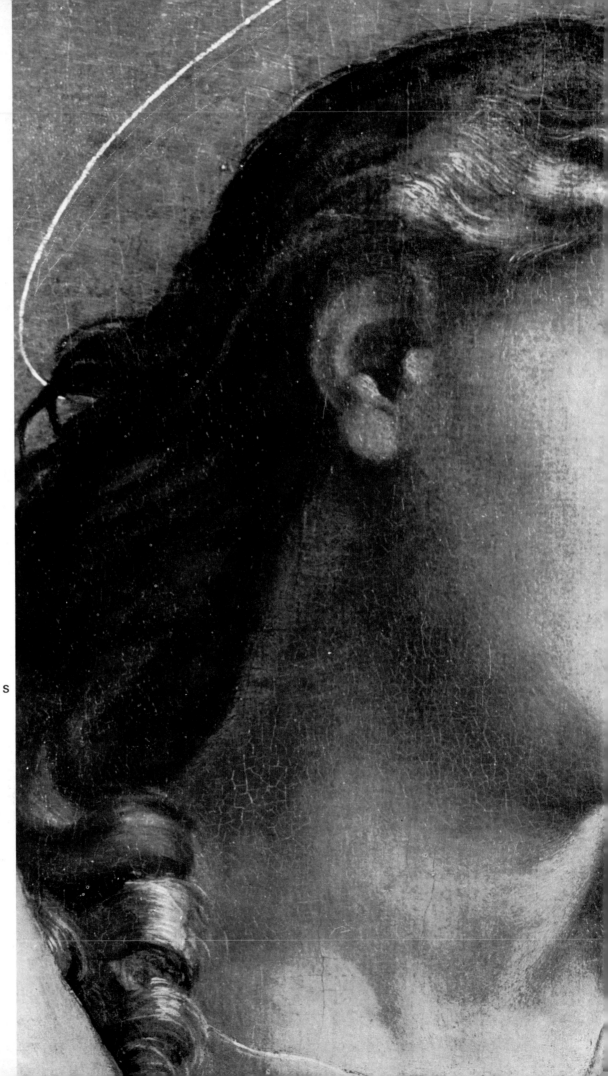

PORTRAITS OF GREATNESS

General Editor
ENZO ORLANDI

Text by
LIANA BORTOLON

Translator
BARBARA PATERSON

Published 1968 by
The Hamlyn Publishing Group Ltd
Hamlyn House, The Centre,
Feltham, Middlesex
© 1965 Arnoldo Mondadori Editore
Translation © 1968 by
The Hamlyn Publishing Group Ltd
Printed in Italy by
Arnoldo Mondadori, Verona

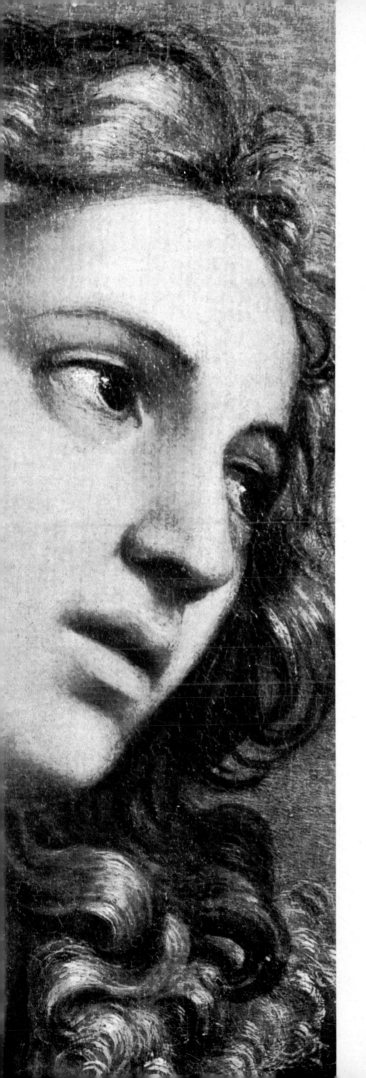

THE LIFE
AND
TIMES OF
RAPHAEL

PAUL HAMLYN
London · New York · Sydney · Toronto

THE COURT OF THE DUKES OF URBINO

A genius can flourish wherever fate happens to locate him. It was nonetheless fortunate for Raphael that he was born in Urbino on April 6, 1483, when the memory of Federico di Montefeltro, who had died only a few months previously, was still very much alive. Federico was a man equally famed for his skill in arms and his love of culture; a famous Renaissance condottiere, and so finished an example of a humanist prince as to arouse the admiration—and perhaps even the envy—of Lorenzo the Magnificent himself. Born in Gubbio in 1422, the son of Count Guidantonio and a woman of pleasure, brought up from his early years in the elegant court of the Gonzagas in Mantua, he became lord of Urbino at the age of 22, succeeding to his half-brother Oddantonio, who had been murdered in a mysterious conspiracy. Federico advanced rapidly, becoming captain-general of the Italian League, and was granted the title of Duke by Papal decree. When he died, the duchy of Urbino was three times as great as it was when he came to power. The palace which he had had built by Luciano di Laurana, and which had cost 200,000 scudi, dominated in every sense a great part of Italy. It contained an unparalleled collection of art treasures. For the silver Federico had paid 40,000 ducats, for the tapestries 10,000 and for the library as much as 230,000. It was at that time the richest in Europe. As became a Renaissance prince, Federico's pride was not unmixed with a touch of vanity. Even though his face had emerged badly damaged from a tournament (with a deeply-gashed nose and the right eye missing), he enjoyed posing for painters. In the portrait on the right, painted by the Spaniard Pedro de Berruguete, the Duke has beside him, loaded with jewels, his small son Guidobaldo, who succeeded him at the age of ten in 1482. Federico is thrusting his left leg forward to show the Order of the Garter bound beneath his knee: he holds a huge book in his hands to bear witness to his fame as a man of letters, and, over his armour, he wears the red mantle of the Order of the Ermine Collar. "A clear crystal light seems to radiate from the Duke," wrote his contemporaries; and it was in this light that the youthful Raphael grew up and began his career as a painter. It was a stimulating environment for a young artist, and particularly for one of genius.

Left: the famous portrait which the Duke of Urbino, Federico di Montefeltro, commissioned from the Spaniard Pedro de Berruguete to hang in his little studio as part of a series of famous men. Here on the right are some works, still to be seen in the Palazzo Ducale in Urbino, by those great painters who were attracted first by Federico, and then by Guidobaldo to their court, which was in those days, and with some justification, known as "l'Asil delle Muse"—"the Haven of the Muses".

These were the surroundings which encouraged the first flowerings of Bramante's genius, and in the same atmosphere Raphael grew up and worked. The pictures which he left at Urbino, and the portraits he painted of the people there, demonstrate how thoroughly he had absorbed the invaluable teachings of the artists who were working in that court, where life, under the guidance of the witty and learned Baldassare Castiglione was gay without being pompous.

All the great painters of the time met and painted at Urbino: from Piero della Francesca, who in his "Flagellation", top, included a group showing Oddantonio di Montefeltro among the treacherous councillors who caused his death, to Paolo Uccello, among whose works at Urbino the scene, centre, of the "Profanation of the Host" is particularly noteworthy, and to Giusto di Gand, who in his "Communion with the Apostles", right, did not forget to include Duke Federico in his red hat.

HE LEARNED TO PAINT FROM HIS FATHER

Raphael learned to paint in his father's studio. Giovanni Santi was well known to the court of Urbino; the painting of a martyr, right, is his, although for some time it was attributed to Raphael himself. Giovanni came from a family of small farmers and traders which went back to the time of Dante. In his forties he had married the very young and beautiful daughter of an Urbino merchant, Magia Ciarla, who brought him a dowry of at least 150 florins and bore him three children, two of whom died in infancy. The future master of the Renaissance was born in the district of Monte, on the night of April 6 (Good Friday) 1483. His father hopefully gave him the auspicious name of an archangel, but Raphael's childhood was not a happy one. He lost his mother when he was eight, and his father remarried; but Bernardina di Pietro was never a good step-mother to him. So the boy learned early to be independent, and he was fortunate that his natural inclination urged him towards the magic world of painting. In August 1494 his father died, recommending his son to the Duchess Elisabetta Gonzaga, wife of Duke Guidobaldo di Montefeltro. At this time of grief, Raphael found himself drawn to a 25-year-old Urbino painter, Timoteo Viti, a lively character, popular at court. Then in 1495 came the fateful encounter with Perugino. Perugino, who was then and still is considered a great master, had a very famous studio, crowded with students because he had more than enough work for everyone. But no sooner had Raphael started to paint with him than something extraordinary took place: Perugino, as though under the other's influence, began to paint like Raphael himself, while his pupil, who was there with quite other intentions, struggled to imitate his teacher as closely as he could. As a result the two worked together hand-in-glove, and later the young man had to fight to free himself from what Vasari, in his "Lives of the Painters", called "the cloying influence" of Perugino. But Raphael's genius was open-minded, and he was capable of absorbing influences from other contemporary painters as well. So that, for example, the element of fantasy and romance in Pinturicchio's work leaves its impression on Raphael's paintings in the form of an additional touch of poetry.

Left: "A Martyr" by Giovanni Santi, Raphael's father. Below: Pietro Vanucci, called Perugino, in a portrait attributed to Raphael. At this time Perugino was one of the most courted painters in Italy. Not long afterwards, however, in the Vatican in Rome, he was set aside to make room for the young Raphael, his one-time pupil.

Above right: this altarpiece, which shows "The Virgin with St. Sebastian and St. John", is the work of Timoteo Viti, Raphael's friend and contemporary, and later his collaborator in Rome.

Immediately above: a detail from the painting "Pius II Leaves for the Council of Baste", carried out by Pinturicchio for the Piccolomini Library at Siena with the probable assistance of Raphael.

THE ANXIETIES AND DREAMS OF YOUTH

When he left Perugino's school to start on his own, Raphael painted, before he was 20, four small but very accomplished pictures which mirror an ideal of classical beauty typical of the age. "The Knight's Dream" at the foot of this page, depicts an allegory. A sleeping knight is roused by two ladies: one is Virtue, offering a sword and a book, and the other is Voluptuousness, holding out a bunch of flowers. Some critics have seen this picture as a spiritual self-portrait of Raphael, torn always between two opposing types of women: between the gentle and innocent girl whom he much later accepted against his wishes as his betrothed, Maria Bibbiena, who died only a few months before him at the age of 18, and the passionate Fornarina, who remained with him all his life. Certainly Raphael had no desire to marry. In a letter to his mother's brother, Simone Ciarla, in 1514, he congratulated himself on not accepting a suitable girl from Urbino suggested by his uncle, because this would leave him free to dedicate himself entirely to his art—and to profit exceedingly from it. In the same letter he spoke highly of dowries in general, and in particular of the dowry of Maria, niece of the celebrated Cardinal Bibbiena ("3,000 gold scudi; and 100 scudi in Rome are worth 200 in Urbino"); but he was to seize one pretext after another to postpone marriage with her. That he was, however, far from insensible to feminine charms can be seen from the little picture at the top, "The Three Graces", with their well-proportioned and neatly-rounded bodies. The other two small pictures, carried out probably for Duke Guidobaldo di Montefeltro, are both of warriors. In the first we see "St. Michael and the Demon", in which the archangel, against a Dantesque background, attacks the devil with his sword. In Raphael's treatment of the curious monsters in this scene, two of which are shown in black and white detail, he is thought to have been influenced by the paintings of the Flemish artist Hieronymus Bosch. This somewhat macabre strain of fantasy does not reappear in his later works. In the second picture, "St. George and the Dragon", the saint rears up, sword in hand, on his horse, which has still—with its rather wooden proportions—much in common with the horses of Paolo Uccello.

"St. Michael and the Demon" and
"St. George and the Dragon" also
formed a diptych, painted in
1504–5. In the seventeenth century
they belonged to Charles I; they
were then acquired by Cardinal
Mazarin and sold by his heirs to
Louis XIV. They are today in the
Louvre, Paris. In the centre is a
detail from "St. Michael and the
Demon".

9

HIS FIRST MASTERPIECE AT 21

Below left: "The Betrothal", in Caen, painted by Perugino; and the little Church of St. Peter in Montorio, designed by Bramante, which inspired Raphael in his "Betrothal of the Virgin", opposite, far right. In the detail, below right, are two members of the Albizzini family who commissioned the picture; beneath this is the signature and the date "Raphael Urbinas MDIII". The subject is taken from the Bible: after the High Priest had invited those who aspired to Mary's hand to come before him with dried almond branches, only the one held by Joseph the poorest and humblest, miraculously burst into flower; a clear sign of the will of God.

"The Betrothal of the Virgin" was commissioned from Raphael by the Albizzini family of Citta di Castello, two members of which are included in the painting. The artist, then barely 20 years old, lodged in the sacristy of the church during the time he took to complete the painting. Raphael derived the basic idea for the work from Perugino's "Betrothal"; but, as Bramante had taught him, he succeeded in giving it a more harmonious composition and a greater internal unity while observing a stricter perspective. Painted in oils (the new technique of Flemish origin) "The Betrothal of the Virgin" had an adventurous history. In a letter written in 1571 to the Duke of Urbino, Mons. della Rovere complained of the lack of interest of the grand-daughter who had inherited the Albizzini properties, which might perhaps be considered a partial justification for the Duke of Urbino's attempt to seize the picture and remove it to his palace. But the monks defended the property of their patrons, and "The Betrothal" remained behind the altar right up to the Napoleonic invasion, when the notables of Città di Castello decided to present it to General Lechi. Hastily restored, it was exhibited for some time in the Lechi Palace in Corso Venezia in Milan. Then it was bought for 50,000 lire by a Milanese nobleman, Giacomo Sannazzari, who in 1804 left it to the Ospedale Maggiore, who then sold it to the government of the time. It then passed to the Minister of Finance, and along with four other masterpieces was sold for 83,000 lire to the Brera Academy, where it remains today—although in 1859 it narrowly escaped being sent to France through an excess of patriotic zeal. This masterpiece continued to arouse comment: when the over-enthusiastic restorations of the nineteenth-century painter Giuseppe Molteni threatened to overshadow it, and again recently, when, in June 1958, it was attacked and badly gashed with a hammer and chisel by a mentally unbalanced visitor to the gallery. Today, having been skilfully restored by Mauro Pelliccioli, "The Betrothal of the Virgin" is carefully protected behind thick glass, and may be admired in the Brera Gallery, hanging side by side with a Piero della Francesca "Madonna", which includes a further portrait of the Duke Federico di Montefeltro, the ruler and artistic patron of Urbino.

THE SWEET SERENITY OF MOTHERHOOD

The "Madonna del Cardellino" was painted about 1506 for a friend (mentioned by Vasari but otherwise unknown), Vincenzo Nasi, to celebrate his wedding. In November 1547 the picture was left in an appalling state following the collapse of the Nasi residence, and it had to be restored. This was done, not too skilfully, by Michele di Ridolfo del Ghirlandaio. Vertical cracks are still clearly visible; it has been crudely retouched, and the whole surface has darkened. It came to the Uffizi in 1666 in the collection of Cardinal Carlo de' Medici.

During the time he spent in Florence and in his early years in Rome, Raphael in his canvases extols the sweetness and loving-kindness of the mother Mary. The theme of the Madonna and Child, often accompanied by St. John, has made him a popular artist right up to our own time, both because of the human tenderness he managed to express and for the new ideal of feminine beauty he created, suffusing his figures with a soft light which recalls Leonardo. But there is something more to it than this. With his increased knowledge of composition he placed his divine figures so as to create a pyramidal shape and thus enclose the whole scene in an ideal geometric figure. The most popular version is certainly the "Madonna del Cardellino" shown here, which closely follows this general pattern with the additional feature of the book in Mary's hand: an element which deliberately interrupts the symmetry without disturbing the harmonious flow of the three figures as they gently incline towards each other. In the following pages there are other examples of compositions of this kind, each enriched by new elements. All these works were carried out between 1505–11; that is, between Raphael's Florentine period (after being introduced to the chief magistrate Pier Soderini, the great patron of the arts, in a letter from Giovanna Feltria, wife of one of the della Rovere) and the decoration of the Vatican Stanze commissioned by Julius II. With his religious temperament, his good heart and his excellent relations with the papal court, Raphael hoped at one point in his life, not without justification, to be named a cardinal. This was in fact suggested by Leo X's advisers, and by Bibbiena in particular. Vasari writes, "having for so many years served the Court and seeing Leo X in his debt for a goodly sum, he was encouraged to believe that, as a just reward for his labours and his many virtues, the Pope would give him a red hat". And he would most probably have become a cardinal had he not died an early death at the age of only 37. This is not as surprising as it sounds if we remember that at the time even a citizen who had never taken holy orders of any kind could be named cardinal by the Pope. It was required, however, that he should be unmarried and to be well-known for piety and good moral character.

Opposite: "*The Madonna del Baldacchino*", *a huge canvas which hangs in the Palazzo Pitti in Florence. To the left of the Virgin's throne stand St. Peter and St. Bruno; to the right, St. Joseph and St. Augustine in his bishop's robes. Raphael began this work in 1506 for the altar of the Dei family in the Church of San Spirito in Florence, and left it unfinished when he departed for Rome. In 1700 the painter Niccolò Cassana was entrusted by Ferdinando de' Medici with the task of completing it. The pyramidal structure is sharply defined, with embellishments such as the two angels flying round the canopy and repeating the circular movement of the apse.*

Above left: the "Belle Jardinière", commissioned in 1507 for Siena by Filippo Sergardi, and left unfinished on Raphael's departure for Rome. This too was entrusted to Michele di Ridolfo del Ghirlandaio, who was responsible for the rather hard blue of the mantle. It was bought by François I of France. "The Madonna of the Field" is another classic example of the pyramidal construction, rising to its apex above the Virgin's head. The landscape has echoes of the countryside round Lake Trasimene near Passignano. On the Virgin's mantle, which is a more characteristic deep blue, can be seen the date: MDVI. This work is now in the Kunsthistorisches Museum, Vienna.

15

HIS METICULOUS AND DETAILED STUDIES

Before taking brush in hand Raphael insisted, as a preliminary and indispensable stage, on making careful drawings from every angle of all the details he was to treat. Here, for example, Raphael was experimenting to find the happiest way to group Mary and the Child together. These date from an already mature stage of Raphael's art. The Child, who to begin with was shown sedately sitting in his mother's lap, has now become a lively, restless creature often on the point of escaping from his mother's embrace, leaning light-heartedly away from her. Below left is his study for the Bridgewater "Madonna" with the various solutions he was working out. In the

centre, the Child from the "Belle Jardinière". On the right, the Alba "Madonna", a masterly composition within a circle. For drawing materials Raphael used pencil, pen and ink, line and wash, charcoal and white lead. 53 magnificent pages from his "Book of Drawings" are preserved in the Venice Academy.

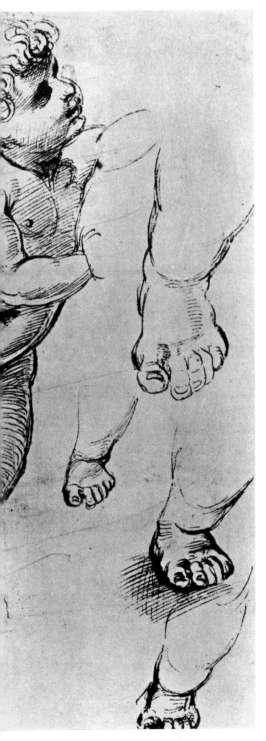

A DISTURBING MYSTERY

During his stay in Rome, in the service first of Julius II and then of Leo X, while painting the Vatican Stanze, Raphael was feverishly busy carrying out ever more frequent commissions. Architect of St. Peter's after Bramante, fully occupied with the frescoes for the Stanze and the Farnesina, involved in a series of portraits of famous people, archaeologist to the Pope, sculptor, designer of tapestries and mosaics, Raphael had only brief moments of respite, capably assisted though he was by his pupils Giulio Romano, Francesco Penni, Pierin del Vaga, and many others. ("He never went to court," reported Vasari, "without being accompanied by fifty painters of good repute.") Often he had to confine himself to planning a work which his pupils then executed under his guidance. The theme of the Virgin, however, continued to fascinate him, and in his moments of peace and serenity he succeeded in painting a series of Madonnas which show a new side to his character. Indeed in the works of this Roman period (painted between 1514–6) Raphael seems to transcend the idyllic warmth and humanity of his Florentine Madonnas—to stress more strongly the innate mystery of the motherhood of God. It might perhaps be suggested that they embody Raphael's own human experiences. There is no longer any landscape to distract the spectator's attention. The whole interest is concentrated on the figures. The picture on the right is the "Madonna della Tenda", now in Munich, and itself probably a preparatory study for the following work, the "Madonna della Seggiola", now in the Pitti Gallery in Florence. In the first, there is a glimpse of sky beyond the tent which gives the painting its name. In the next picture there is not even this visual possibility of escape. The Mother and Child form a still more tightly enclosed group, which indeed almost excludes the little St. John. It is a particularly formal composition, in which even the right foot of the Child plays its part in the circular movement of the design. But there is something even more interesting than the austerity of the composition; that is the directness of communication between the spectator and the limpid eyes of Mary and the Child as they look straight out from the canvas, conveying a deep and disquieting sense of mystery.

"The Madonna della Tenda", painted about 1515 or 1516, was apparently at one time in France, although according to some authorities it was kept at the Escorial in Madrid. However, in the early part of the nineteenth century it was bought for £4,000 and taken to England; there it was sold for £5,000 to Prince Ludwig of Bavaria. Today it is in Munich. Quite apart from early retouchings, this picture, measuring 26 ins × 26 ins, has suffered also from lack of care and the ravages of time; but it has always been particularly famous as a typical example of Raphael's painting and has been much copied.

Below: the famous "Madonna della Seggiola", probably painted not long after the "Madonna della Tenda". It is a tondo 28 ins in diameter, painted on wood. The three figures, Mary, the Child, and St. John, are placed in three slightly receding planes to increase the illusion of depth. Not long after Raphael's death, the painting was in the possession of the Medici family. Early in the eighteenth century it passed from the Uffizi to the Pitti: from 1799–1815 it was kept in Paris with the rest of Napoleon's booty. It is now in Florence. In some ways it recalls the tondi of Botticelli, and in the inter-relationship of the figures it resembles some of Michelangelo's work.

Three examples of the Child moving about in his mother's arms. The little picture below, the "Madonna d'Orléans", measuring 12 ins × 8 ins, has been identified as one of the two Virgins which Vasari records were painted by Raphael towards 1507 for Guidobaldo di Montefeltro. It achieves a marvellous harmony through the repetition of the diagonal pose of the two figures and the charm of its colouring. The "Madonna Colonna", centre, today in Berlin, takes its name from the family to which it belonged for some time, and was executed around the same date as the earlier one. Finally, the huge "Madonna di Foligno", right, 10 ft 6 ins × 6 ft 6 ins. It was commissioned as a thanksgiving by the scholar Sigismondo de' Conti (right, kneeling) for the danger he had escaped when a thunderbolt narrowly missed his house. Its composition is formal, with Mary and the Child inside one circle, flanked by the two semicircles of angels and adoring figures.

THE PAGE-BOY
WITH THE HUGE
DARK EYES

The most famous self-portrait by Raphael is the one in the Uffizi, shown on the opposite page. We see the rather idealized face of a man with finely-drawn features, large dark eyes, and hair flowing down to his shoulders. Was Raphael really so personable? At the age of 16 he certainly had the refined and dreamy expression of the boy in the hat in the picture above. But as time went by his features coarsened somewhat. At the age of 20, to judge from a self-portrait which is now in Munich, he must have had a rather rounded face with a slightly flattened nose and a receding chin. To hide this, or to distract from the excessive pallor of his face resulting from the malaria which afflicted him in Rome, Raphael allowed his beard to grow.

Left: Raphael as an adolescent. This drawing is in Oxford. Some have attributed it to Timoteo Viti, but it bears the inscription "Self-portrait of himself when young", which should dispose of any doubts. The subtle play of light and shade is handled with a delicacy typical of Raphael. Above right: this is another self-portrait taken from a painting in the Louvre in which the painter appears at the side of his fencing-master (or perhaps of a pupil, who may be Polidoro da Caravaggio). It dates

from 1518, and depicts the artist when he was already suffering from malaria. Right: this is the best-known self-portrait of Raphael, with its somewhat remote and romantic expression, its delicately-idealized features, large and rather prominent eyes and long flowing page-boy hair. Dating from about 1506, it can be seen today in the Uffizi in Florence. (There is also another self-portrait before he grew a beard, dating from 1504 or 1505, which is in Munich.)

HIS ENORMOUS DEBT TO LEONARDO

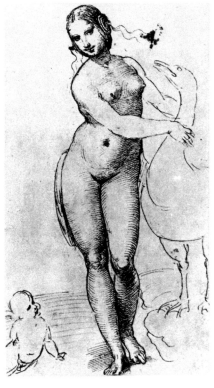

Here are some indications of the bond of ideas which linked Raphael's painting with that of Leonardo. Left: Leonardo's "Leda", which was copied by Raphael in minute detail in his drawing in the Royal Collection, Windsor. Right: Leonardo's "Virgin and St. Anne" (Louvre, Paris) which suggested the composition of Raphael's "Canigiani Holy Family" on the opposite page. In this work, carried out about 1507 for the Florentine Domenico Canigiani, the pyramidal composition is clear from the first glance, built up in turn by other, lesser triangles formed by the various figures. A straight line could be drawn from the foot of the Madonna through to

the white-shawled head of St. Elizabeth, and another triangle could be described following the lines indicated by the hands of the two women, with its apex at the base of the composition. The background was inspired by a northern painter, but the treatment is softer. Raphael's signature runs along the neckline of Mary's gown. This important picture passed from the heirs of Domenico Canigiani at some unknown period to the Medici Family, and from them to the Elector Palatine, Hans William, who married Anna Maria Luis, daughter of Grand Duke Cosimo III. From Düsseldorf it was finally transferred to the Munich Art Gallery in 1801.

Leonardo was about 30 years older than Raphael. Early in the 1500s he was working on the preliminary designs for the "Battle of Anghiari", which was to decorate a wall of the Palazzo Vecchio together with Michelangelo's "Battle of Cascina". The two frescoes were never carried out, but the cartoons alone were enough to inspire an entire generation. Raphael also saw them, and during his stay in Florence he had the opportunity to study them and to meet Leonardo. From him he learned his methods of pyramidal construction, the possibilities of drawing portraits in three-quarter rather than full-face, his translucence, his half-light, the elegance of his hands. Raphael also abandoned Perugino's cross-hatching care for a lively Leonardo-like scribble, all dashes and spirals. Raphael met Leonardo again when the great painter came to Rome at the invitation of Giuliano de' Medici, and was installed in the Villa Belvedere. But the Pope was incapable of appreciating him and allowed him to depart for the French court.

"The Deposition", in the Borghese Gallery in Rome, shows clearly the artistic links between Michelangelo and Raphael. One has only to compare it with the marble *"Pietà"* below and the Doni tondo opposite, both by Michelangelo. *(Look first at the figure of Mary and then at that of the young woman crouched at the right side of "The Deposition" supporting the swooning Virgin.)* From his rival Raphael learned his dramatic sense, the three-dimensional solidity of his figures, his skill at portraying muscles under stress—techniques which he adopted with great skill in his Vatican frescoes. It is interesting to note here that the violent movement of the heads follows a strict rhythmic pattern. The body of Christ marvellously unites the two halves of the composition.

HIS DIFFERENCES
WITH MICHELANGELO

Raphael's admiration extended also to Michelangelo who, however, returned it with open hostility. "Raphael being one day in company with his followers," records one biographer, "he encountered Michelangelo, who asked him: 'Where are you going thus escorted like a lord?' And he retorted, 'And where you, solitary as an executioner?'" But the vigour of Michelangelo's ideas could not help but influence Raphael. While Michelangelo was away from Rome, Julius II succeeded in partially uncovering the roof of the Sistine Chapel, so impatient was he to see the work which had only just been started: Raphael took advantage of this opportunity to study the powerful muscularity of the nudes and the dramatic intensity of the scenes. When Michelangelo heard what had happened he flew into a fearful rage, taking the incident as an open challenge from this young man who dared to pit himself against him. Nonetheless, when an argument arose about the payment for the "Sibyls" painted by Raphael in Santa Maria della Pace, Michelangelo, who had been asked to arbitrate, recognized that the work deserved far more than the price that had been agreed upon, and declared that Raphael should be paid double.

BASIC FRAMEWORK: THE SKELETON

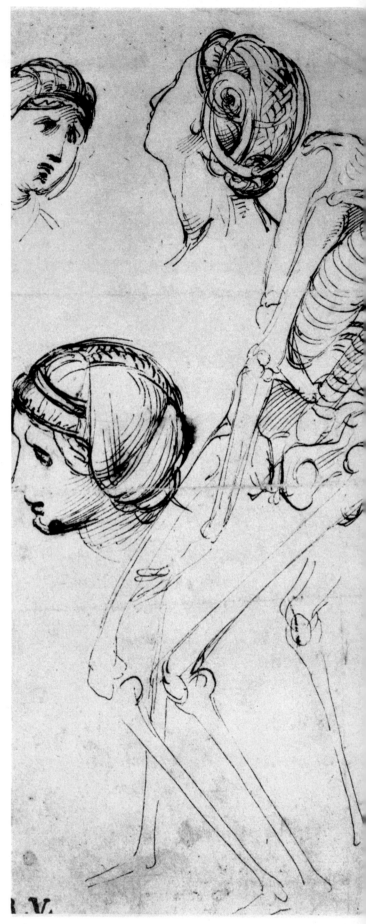

These drawings for "The Deposition", which are among Raphael's most important studies, allow us to examine minutely his technique and attention to detail. Nothing is left to chance, inspiration or improvisation; everything is worked out with the utmost dedication. About 16 preparatory drawings (today scattered between Oxford, London, Paris and Florence) bear witness to the intense preparatory work behind this painting, which was at first conceived as "Mourning over the Dead Christ". In the first sketch, above, the whole scene has already taken shape: the Saviour's body is borne by two men (one of them Nicodemus) whose attitude of strain has already been skilfully worked out. On the right is a rather curious drawing: amid several very elegantly coiffured ladies is a study for the pose of the unconscious Virgin. Like Leonardo, Raphael started by drawing the skeleton itself, in order to be certain of a convincing body, and only then clothed it in flesh and garments. "The Deposition" was carried out in 1507, attested by the Latin inscription on the step at the bottom of the picture, to commemorate a tragic episode in Perugia's history. In August 1500 a nobleman called Grifonetto Baglioni was assassinated in revenge by a member of his own family, who had himself previously escaped from the slaughter ordered by Baglioni to gain power. Atalanta, Baglioni's mother, ordered the work from Raphael so that in Mary's grief her own mourning for her son would be remembered.

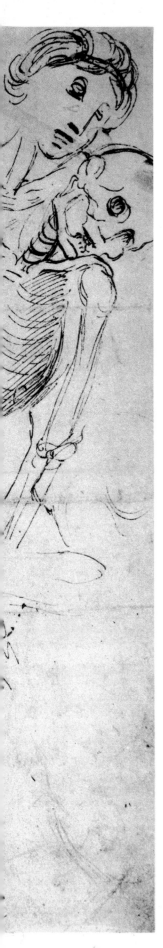

HIS PORTRAITS REVEAL THE GREAT MEN OF HIS AGE

Immediately below: the portrait of Guidobaldo di Montefeltro, today in the Uffizi, painted 1506–7. Below: Cardinal Bibbiena, a picture in the Pitti on which critics hold differing opinions. Some maintain that it owes much to the collaboration of assistants, with the exception of the head, for which Raphael is certainly responsible.

In this singular series of portraits Raphael has rendered immortal the likenesses of the famous men of his time who were drawn to the papal court. Above, next to the cardinal who is described below, is the finely-drawn face with its inner serenity of Guidobaldo di Montefeltro, Duke of Urbino, son of Federico. Guidobaldo had succeeded his father in 1482 at the age of ten, under the regency of his uncle Ottaviano Ubaldini. He had later been forced to abandon Urbino when Duke Valentino, who coveted his duchy, entered the city by treachery. With the election of Giuliano della Rovere to the papacy as Julius II, Guidobaldo regained his duchy and extended his forgiveness to Cesare Borgia. The Duke was never strong in health. When only 20 he suffered from gout and had to spend long periods lying down. He used these intervals for reading and studying, and was immensely learned. Having no children by his wife, Elisabetta Gonzaga, he adopted his sister's son, Francesco Maria della Rovere, who later succeeded him. Guidobaldo, deeply resigned to the woes of this

life, found himself to be—for the times in which he lived—like a piece of fine porcelain surrounded by vessels of bronze. The man wearing the large hat in the black and white picture on the opposite page is Giuliano de' Medici, son of Lorenzo the Magnificent, and the brother of Cardinal Giovanni de' Medici who became Pope Leo X at the age of only 38. Giuliano undoubtedly profited from the complex game of papal nepotism, but he carried with him into the self-indulgent court of Leo X qualities of gentleness and tolerance. Shortly before his death he vainly begged his brother to abstain from his plans for the duchy of Urbino, which he wished to pass on to his own nephew Lorenzo. The third portrait, right, in colour, shows the intelligent and refined face of Baldassare Castiglione, the brilliant Lombard nobleman, who lived for many years at the court of Urbino, where he collected the material for his *Cortegiano* (The Courtier). A skilful diplomat as well as a humanist and scholar, he enjoyed the respect of both Julius II and Leo X, and the friendship of Raphael. This portrait has been

called "the most Renaissance of Renaissance portraits". Let us come back again to Cardinal Bernardo Dovizi, called Bibbiena after his birth-place not far from Arezzo, who was appointed first papal treasurer and then Cardinal by Leo X as a reward for his loyalty to the Medici family. He exercised considerable influence over the papal court, thanks partly to his talents and partly to his ebullient personality. One of his famous tricks was the one he played on the poet Baraballo, who was hitched up onto the back of a white elephant in order to be crowned in Campidoglio, and instead was abruptly "unloaded" to the jeers of the populace. He wrote a comedy, *La Calandria*, performed for the first time before the court of Urbino, and later before the Pope, with great success. The cardinal conceived an admiration for Raphael, and decided that the painter should marry his niece Maria. He employed him to decorate his "hot-house", that is, his bathroom, in the Vatican, with marvellous allegorical figures, which can be seen there still. With his high spirits and lavish generosity, Bibbiena is a typical Renaissance figure.

31

Below: Elisabetta Gonzaga, Duchess of Urbino, who befriended Raphael in his early years. Bottom: Emilia Pia di Montefeltro, the Duchess's friend as well as her niece and executrix of her will. These two portraits, the first in the Uffizi and the second in Baltimore, were painted in 1504 during a brief stay by Raphael in Urbino.

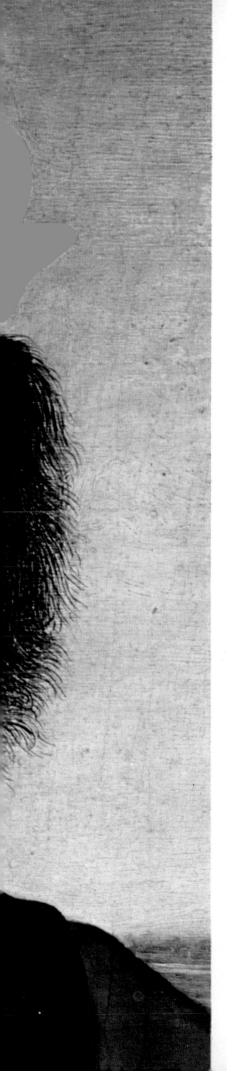

*Below: the first portrait is of
Cardinal Francesco Alidosi, friend
of Julius II. The second is of Fedra
Inghirami, Bishop of Volterra, who
at the time of Leo X was prefect of
the Vatican Library. This portrait is
in the Pitti. An almost identical one
in Boston has aroused many
arguments between critics. Centre:
the head of Angelo Doni.*

Around Raphael moved several people who influenced the way his life took shape. The first was Elisabetta Gonzaga, the wife of Duke Guidobaldo di Montefeltro: it was to her that Giovanni Santi on his death bed recommended his young son. The Duchess nurtured in Urbino that tranquil, intellectual atmosphere of a Court of Chivalry which attracted the foremost personalities of the time. Below her portrait is that of Emilia Pia di Montefeltro, her friend, the natural daughter of her brother-in-law. These two faces share certain similarities, both in the directness of their gaze and their almost stylized features (their absence of eyebrows is due to the current mode for shaving them off). In the centre, a man whom Raphael met in Florence: Angelo Doni, who is remembered today both for this painting and a Madonna, now in the Uffizi in Florence (the "Doni Madonna"), and also because of a comment by Vasari, who reported that Doni, whilst admiring beautiful things, spent willingly but as sparingly as he could. Rich at that time, but not excessively open-handed, he married in 1503 the 14-year-old Maddalena Strozzi, whose portrait can be seen a few pages further on. Finally, on the right, two prelates of the papal court, who have given the artist ample opportunity to display his psychological insight. Indeed, in the first portrait, which is considered to be that of Francesco Alidosi, Cardinal of Pavia, the intimate friend and confidant of Julius II, there can be glimpsed beneath the slight smile the calculating and ambitious character he really was. The cardinal is known to have come into conflict with Francesco Maria della Rovere, the Pope's nephew, during the occupation of Bologna, because he had abandoned his city to the opposing faction. At Ravenna, in the presence of the Pope himself, they began heatedly to blame each other for the loss of Bologna until the Duke della Rovere, beside himself with rage, ran him through with his sword before the eyes of his following. Below, Bishop Inghirami, called Fedra, prefect of the Vatican library and a friend of Leo X, who, it seems, personally commissioned this portrait from Raphael. Plump, with a slight squint, and not without a certain kindly dignity, Inghirami seems to us the typical Renaissance scholar, brought vividly to life by Raphael's skilful portraiture.

A FAMILIAR WORLD

Raphael never travelled far from his native city. His early journeys in Perugino's following took him no further than the borders of Umbria and the Marches. Once, perhaps, he accompanied him as far as Florence, and later he spent several years here. For the backgrounds of his pictures—and especially of his Madonnas—Raphael chose familiar landscapes which recall the countryside round Urbino or the romantic shores of Lake Trasimene, the gentle Tuscan plains or castles perched on hillsides: a world made to human measurements, evocative also to those patrons who themselves lived in the cities of central Italy. More rarely he sought inspiration from imaginary landscapes, or added elements derived from the subject of the work.

Three of Raphael's works with their backgrounds: the "Madonna del Cardellino", the "Madonna di Foligno", and the "Canigiani Holy Family". The first is set in an idyllic and spring-like world, as can be seen from the detail shown left: fields, trees, a stream under an arched bridge. It gives the impression of being both familiar and recognizable. In small detail on the opposite page, a part of Foligno is lit by a streak of light—the thunderbolt which struck the surrounding dwellings leaving miraculously unharmed the house of Sigismondo de' Conti, who commissioned the picture. Below: a village and a fortified city, probably of northern inspiration.

THE HANDS
ARE PORTRAITS
IN THEMSELVES

Depicting hands was such a severe test of an artist's skill that mediocre painters were reluctant even to attempt them, while those more highly skilled charged more for it. Raphael was determined to reveal in every part of the painting the character of the person he was portraying. Thus from the architecture of the head, through the geometry of the clothes, to the psychological revelation of the hands, his paintings never show any signs of haste, fatigue or uncertainty. Below are the hands of Leonardo's "Mona Lisa" to which Raphael always returned for inspiration. To the right are two of the most beautiful women he painted, together with the details of their hands. Above are the hands of the "Muta", the unknown lady from the painting in the ducal palace in Urbino; below, those of "Maddalena Doni", from the painting which is today in the Pitti in Florence. The hands of the first, slim, sensitive, spiritual, complement the self-possessed, almost remote person this unknown woman seems to be. They are posed along an imaginary diagonal running from the tip of the forefinger of the left hand to the knuckles of the right and continued by the knot of velvet ribbon at the waist. The woman below, Maddalena Strozzi, who married Angelo Doni, was fair and opulent: and her hands, plump and bejewelled, creating an oval shape, are a perfect reflection of the characteristics visible elsewhere. It is interesting to contrast the personalities expressed by the hands of the two portraits. Those of the rich merchant's wife in fact tell us far more about her character than does the unemotional and unmoved expression of her face.

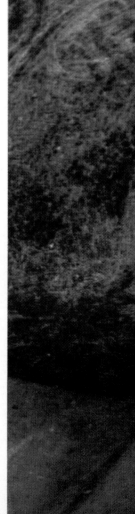

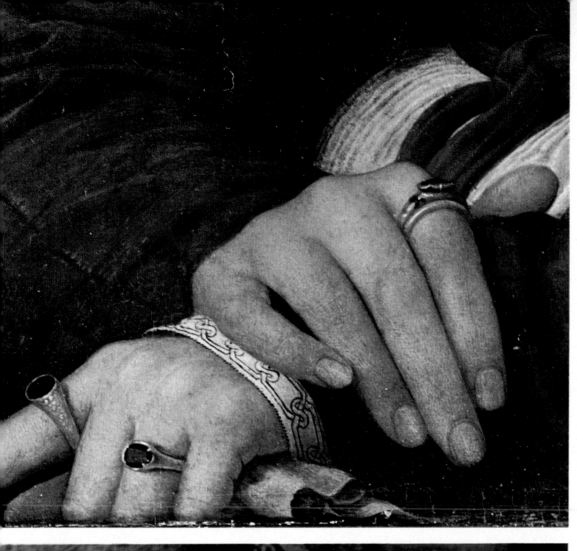

Above: "La Muta", also called "The Lady in Green" from the colour of her dress, painted probably in 1507. Below: Maddalena Doni, in the portrait which Raphael painted together with that of her husband, which is shown on page 32.

STILL-LIFES

"Leo X with Two Cardinals" was painted in 1518. We know that the cardinals were Giulio de' Medici and Luigi di Rossi. Today in the Uffizi, this painting never left the Medici family. It seems that two copies were made, one by Andrea del Sarto, now in Naples, and one by Vasari, now in England.
"St. Cecilia", in the Bologna

Museum, was sent by Raphael to his close friend the painter Francesco Francia so that he could give it to Elena dall' Olio, who had commissioned it, and who paid him 1,000 gold scudi for it. Francia found it so perfect that he lost all confidence in his own art and died not long afterwards of a broken heart.

In some of the details of his pictures, Raphael is daringly in advance of his time. If, for example, we pause to scrutinize the painting of Leo X in his portrait with two cardinals, and the ground at the feet of St. Cecilia, we can already discern hints of the Baroque era, which was indeed to elevate still life to the status of a theme rather than of an adjunct to a painting. In the first painting, Raphael has abandoned himself to the pleasures of virtuosity, arranging to marvellous effect a book illuminated on parchment, a lens and a chased silver bell. At the feet of St. Cecilia, the arrangement of musical instruments—viola, flutes, tambourines and triangle—seems to anticipate the seventeenth-century compositions of the painter Bachenis, who was to specialize in still-lifes with musical instruments.

THE DIVINE STAGE-DESIGNER

One of Raphael's most theatrical works is the Sistine "Madonna", painted when his art was already fully mature. Mary, with the Child in her arms, appears between draperies which sweep back to reveal a cloud-dappled sky. To the right is St. Cecilia, or (according to Vasari) St. Barbara, because of the tower which can be glimpsed behind her shoulders, and for which Eleonora Gonzaga posed. On the left is St. Sixtus with his white alb beneath a damask cope, which some critics have thought to be yet another likeness of Julius II. The two pensive cupids at the base of the picture seem, according to some authorities, to be a later addition to the picture, though still painted by Raphael. In the iconography generally adopted by Raphael this portrayal of Mary is somewhat exceptional. Instead of the fair and gentle beauties of his Florentine period, we find ourselves face to face with a superb dark-haired woman, intensely expressive, a real and very human mother. It seems that the original for this Mary was the famous Fornarina. La Fornarina—the baker's daughter—was Margherita Luti, the young daughter of a Trastevere baker of Siennese descent who was much courted by the young men of her quarter. Raphael was in love with her and often, while in the middle of painting his frescoes in the Farnesina—Agostino Chigi's palace on the banks of the Tiber—he would break off his work to rush down to the girl's house, the prey to sudden jealousy. It seems that at one time Raphael was rushing off so often from the palace scaffolding that Agostino Chigi, concerned because the frescoes were making such slow progress, induced la Fornarina to come and live in the palace so that the painter would not need to tear himself away. In the following pages can be seen a series of cupids and cherubs which form part of the cycle "The Triumph of Galatea" and "The Story of Psyche" that Raphael painted on the walls and ceilings of the Farnesina palace, where they are still to be seen. When we look at the Sistine Madonna, we are confronted with two of the most moving and unforgettable faces in all painting. Either because of the tender and loving expression on the face of this much-loved woman, or perhaps through one of those small miracles which only great painters can achieve, this is surely one of Raphael's most haunting works.

Above : one of the most famous and perhaps the most loved of Raphael's works, the Sistine "Madonna". Mary and the Child create an image of touching tenderness and great vitality. Their figures are enclosed in a kind of ellipse emphasized by her mantle. The whole scene has been set with great skill, seen in the sweep of the draperies, the flow of the garments, and in the placing and foreshortening of the figures on each side. It is one of his rare paintings on canvas, perhaps because it was also intended to be used as a banner in processions. Painted about 1516 (or perhaps, according to other critics, 1513–4) this picture was commissioned by the black monks of the chapel of St. Sixtus at Piacenza, and sold by their successors to Augustus III, Elector of Saxony. Today it is in the Dresden Museum.

40

PAGAN CUPIDS AND HEAVENLY CHERUBS

A series of puckish cupids from "The Triumph of Galatea", a fresco in the palace of Agostino Chigi in Rome, and partly executed by Raphael's pupil, Giulio Romano. Agostino Chigi, a famous Siennese banker, was reputed the richest man of his day. He had an income of 70,000 gold florins, he kept a lavish household, he employed 20,000 people, and he entertained on an extravagant scale. On one occasion he held a great banquet at which his guests ate from silver plates. At the end of each course, to the astonishment of the company, the plates were tossed into the Tiber. Chigi had taken the precaution, however, of spreading nets in the river beforehand, so that after the departure of the guests his servants were able to pull

42

them safely back to shore. After the cupids in the classical tradition with their tridents, pipes and bows, here are the Christian cherubs—who look fairly similar. The two thoughtful cherubs leaning on an imaginary window-sill come from the Sistine "Madonna". Faced with the work of Raphael's maturity, even his fiercest rivals were forced to pay homage. When Chigi's treasurer baulked at paying 500 ducats for "Sibyls and Angels" painted in Santa Maria della Pace in Rome, Michelangelo was asked to arbitrate. Though the dour and eccentric old genius had no love for his fêted young rival, he was so impressed by the beauty of the work that he declared that Raphael should be paid twice the amount that had been agreed upon.

JULIAN II AND LEO X

Raphael's fortunes owed much to the patronage of two great Popes, Julius II and Leo X. The first, formerly Cardinal Giuliano della Rovere, had assumed the name of Julius II on becoming Pope in 1503. When Raphael first met him, the best artists of the time—Sodoma, Luca Signorelli, Baldassare Peruzzi and Perugino—were working for him, painting frescoes in the new rooms which he had taken over to avoid living in the old Borgia apartments; Michelangelo had been employed to decorate the Sistine Chapel, and Leonardo to work on problems of engineering and hydraulics. In 1506 the first stone of the great new Church of St. Peter had already been laid, and the work entrusted to Bramante. When the famous architect introduced Raphael, then 25 years old, as a distant relative, Julius II was at first won over more by the young man's charm than by his talent. Later, however, when he saw the initial stages of "The Disputation of the Sacraments" in the Stanza della Segnatura, the Pope impulsively ordered that the other painters should be dismissed and their work erased, and turned the entire project over to Raphael. Julius II died during the night of February 22, 1513, and three weeks later Cardinal Giovanni de' Medici, son of Lorenzo the Magnificent, was elected Pope at the age of 38 with the title of Leo X. The new Pope had no desire to wage war like his predecessor, but like his father before him he was a patron of the arts and like him too wished to leave a memorial to his own greatness. "Let us profit from the papacy since God has given it to us," he remarked to his brother Giuliano. So Leo X, too, showed himself to be a good friend to artists. He prized both Michelangelo—whose awkward character often aroused his displeasure—and Raphael, whose pleasant and witty conversation he much enjoyed. An example of Raphael's wit is seen in an anecdote which tells how one day two cardinals were complaining that the faces of Peter and Paul in one of his paintings were too highly-coloured. "I did that on purpose, my lords," replied Raphael, "for I find it highly probable that even in heaven St. Peter and St. Paul must blush for shame to see the Church ruled by men like you." Leo X, who had inherited his great father's courtly and intelligent love of wit, was much amused by this reply.

44

Left: in this detail from "The Expulsion of Heliodorus" the most prominent figure is that of Julius II, seated in his papal sedan; the Pope had sworn never to shave his beard again until he had defeated the French. Portrayed as the two litter bearers are Giulio Romano and the engraver Marcantonio Raimondi. During the Sack of Rome in 1527 the Spanish encamped in the city caused considerable damage to this fresco by lighting a fire beneath it. Below: a detail from "The Meeting of Attila and St. Leo", carried out in 1514 just at the time of the change of Popes. There are two portraits of Leo X. The fresco, which had been planned while Julius III was still alive, had only just been begun when Leo X became Pope; so Raphael, who had already drawn Giovanni de' Medici as the figure on the left, painted him again as Pope in the place of Julius II. The man holding the Pope's stirrup is Serapica, Leo X's personal servant, who was much loved in his time.

THE TRIUMPH OF THE TRUE FAITH

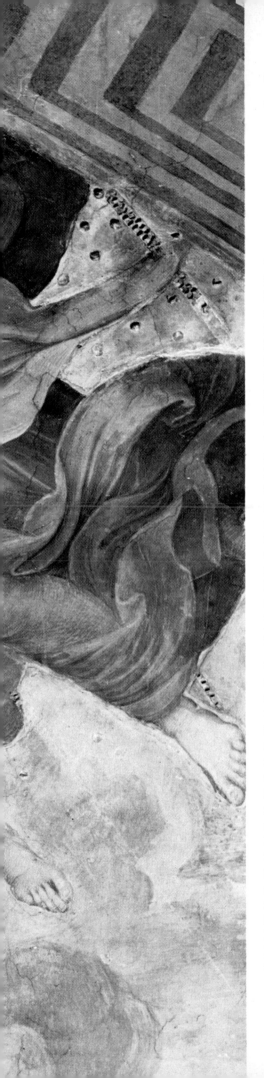

The Stanza della Segnatura (Room of the Signatories) in the Vatican probably owes its name either to its being the meeting-place of the church tribunal of the same name or, according to some authorities, to the fact that it was here that the Pope signed the papal briefs. This room was originally intended, however, to house Julius II's library, and its decoration, begun in 1508, was the first work on which Raphael started soon after arriving from Florence. He left here four testimonies to the perfection of his art: the "Disputá", "The School of Athens", "Parnassus" and "The Virtues". The first three of these can be seen here and in the following pages. The first two, inspired by Julius II himself, were to exalt the victory of the true faith and the triumph of philosophy and science; the third was to be in praise of poetry. Following one of the principles of Platonic philosophy, one of the main sources of the Renaissance, the figurative arts are not praised among the others since they were not considered among the great creations of the human spirit. Raphael therefore confined himself to disguising as ancient philosophers those great masters who were his contemporaries. Plato has the face of Leonardo, Heraclitus that of Michelangelo, Euclid, "the human compass", that of Bramante. Here on the left is a detail from the "Disputá", three superb angels gliding through the sky; its border of clouds divides the heavens with their sacred inhabitants from the earthly realms swarming with men, many of whom are easily recognizable. A marvellous piece of stage-setting, but lacking perhaps, according to some critics, any deep sense of religious faith—which was in any case alien to the spirit of the sixteenth century. So much so that during those years an austere German monk, Martin Luther, appalled at the ostentation and corruption of the papal court itself during his visit to Rome in 1510, was in the throes of working out his theses, which were to be the inspiration of that gigantic reformation which would turn Christendom upside down and put an end to that era of magnificence and munificence of discovery and artistic ferment, an era in which men set the achievements of patrons such as Leo X and painters such as Raphael, who was Luther's contemporary, at more value than religious devotion.

Above: a detail from "The School of Athens", in the Room of the Signatories in the Vatican, showing the two portraits (side by side) of Raphael and Sodoma, his predecessor and collaborator in the paintings of the Vatican Rooms. Left: a detail from the "Disputá".

The "Disputá":
on the left Bramante
can be seen leaning
towards a young man
who is probably
Francesco Maria
della Rovere, the
Pope's nephew.

49

"The School of Athens": in the centre are the two most important Greek philosophers of Antiquity, Plato and Aristotle. Plato, pointing to the sky, is a portrait of Leonardo. Michelangelo is drawn as the brooding Heraclitus at the very front of the picture. On the right, busy measuring a geometric figure, is another picture of Bramante.

50

IN PRAISE
OF POETRY

Poetry also received its allocation of praise on the walls of the Stanza della Segnatura, according to the theme worked out by Julius II. On a hilly and tree-clad Parnassus, 28 muses and poets are gathered together around Apollo who, in the centre beside the waters of Castalia, is sweetly playing his violin instead of the traditional lyre. Begun in 1510 and finished within a year, "Parnassus" reveals that passion for and study of classical antiquity which led Leo X, in a decree dated August 7, 1515, to name Raphael "Custodian of Roman antiquities", and to charge him with "revealing ancient Rome anew". The Pope was deeply concerned to protect the precious ruins from the depredations and spoliation of the "wicked and impious barbarians" who risked destroying them completely. (Some Roman nobles stole blocks of ancient stone and used them to build their palaces.) Raphael set himself the task of working out the plan of imperial Rome; for the reliefs, which he made himself, he used a kind of squaring-up device. The central point was usually the Domus Aurea, which still bears the signatures of his pupils on its walls.

Above: the fresco "Parnassus". Right: a detail from the crowd of poets. In the lower group are Alcaeus, Corinna, Petrarch, Anacreon and Sappho (who can just be glimpsed holding a scroll). Seated above is the Roman Aeneas, intent on transcribing the lines which the figure of the blind Homer is declaiming as he strides forward during a bout of inspiration. This white-bearded head is taken from the Laocöon retrieved not long before from a vineyard near Rome. Just beside him is Dante: towards him turns Virgil, standing slightly behind. The musical instruments which the muses are holding are copied from the so-called Tomb of the Muses in the National Museum in Rome.

THE PROBLEM OF LIGHT

"The Deliverance of St. Peter" offers the solution to another painting problem, handled by Raphael with a genius well in advance of his time and which already anticipates the work of Caravaggio and Rembrandt: the treatment of light and shade. This fresco is in the Stanza di Eliodoro together with "The Expulsion of Heliodorus" (which gives the room its name), "The Mass at Bolsena" and "The Meeting of Attila". "The Deliverance" covers the wall where Piero della Francesca's earlier painting had been erased. The subject is taken from the account in the Acts of the Apostles, which tells how St. Peter, imprisoned in Jerusalem saw in a dream an angel who released him while the guards slumbered: and how, when he awoke, he found himself miraculously released from his prison. The fresco shows simultaneously the two stages of the story. On the architrave of the window are two *trompe l'oeil* plaques with the inscription: "Leo Pont. Max. ann. Christ. MDXIIII Pontificat. sui II". In his treatment of the reflection of light from the guards' armour, he was well in advance of his time.

Above: the fresco of "The Deliverance of St. Peter", a detail of which appears opposite. The darkness of the prison grating is calculated to accentuate the brilliance of the vision of the angel, which is at the same time reflected by the guards' armour.
Unique among Renaissance paintings, in this work there are five sources of light: the moon, the dawn, the torch, and the two figures of the angel. The impression of night probably owes something to Piero della Francesca's "Vision of Constantine". The handling of the liberated St. Peter also recalls Masaccio. A great many paintings showing light reflecting from armour were inspired by the play of light and shade in this picture.

THE PURITY OF HIS COLOURS

On the wall where some years previously Bramante had portrayed several condottieri, Raphael, still in the Stanza di Eliodoro, painted his fresco "The Mass of Bolsena", showing a curious episode which had taken place long before in 1263. In that year a Bohemian priest on his way to Rome had stopped to celebrate mass on the tomb of St. Christina at Bolsena. Doubtful at the time about the truth of the Eucharist, he suddenly saw the consecrated wafer begin to drip blood. This miracle gave rise the following year to the decree by which Urban IV instituted the feast of Corpus Domini (to which Julius II was much devoted). Julius II chose this theme to pay homage to the memory of Urban IV, the initiator of the cult of Corpus Domini, and to celebrate the power of the Church, which had emerged unscathed from the Lateran Council begun in 1512. The purity of the colours in this fresco seem to anticipate the work of the Venetian colourists, with their extreme realism and intensity, and especially to the harmonious paintings of Lorenzo Lotto. Once again, we see how greatly Raphael influenced his successors.

Among the people portrayed in "The Mass of Bolsena", painted about 1512, is Julius II, immediately recognizable as the old man kneeling before the altar. The prelate standing a little way behind him, with his hands crossed on his chest, is probably Cardinal Riario: the one with his hands joined in prayer is Cardinal Sangiorgio. Especially noteworthy is the contrast between the fever of emotion which runs through the left-hand side of the scene and the serenity of the right. Even the candles are stirred by the wind in the first part, but burn without a flicker in the second. Right: a well-preserved detail from the group of Swiss Guards. The rest of the painting has been extensively retouched.

HIS SENSE
OF DRAMA

The story of the expulsion of Heliodorus from the temple of Jerusalem, which was later also to inspire one of Delacroix's murals, is the theme of the great fresco which was the first to be painted in the Stanza di Eliodoro. The choice of scene has given the painter the opportunity to demonstrate the intensely dramatic quality of his art. Heliodorus had succeeded in penetrating the temple to plunder the sacred treasure, despite the pleas of the high priest (here shown kneeling before the altar). But the sacrilegious rogue was struck down with his loot by a heavenly warrior and two other divine messengers. Julius II looks on as the scene takes place: by it the Pope wished to allude to the inviolability of the temporal power of the Church and to its victory over those who would usurp Church possessions. For the fresco, Raphael for the first time examines the possibilities of using light to bind together through the different planes and perspectives the various elements of the composition. This problem was to fascinate the painters of the following centuries, even down to the present day. Here, especially on the right-hand side of the painting, it has not been too skilfully handled, because it is partly the work of pupils and assistants.

Above: "The Expulsion of Heliodorus", with its interesting treatment of perspective. Right: the dramatic detail showing the terror of the sacrilegious thieves as they are surprised by the avenging angels. The fresco was carried out between 1511 and 1512 (though Raphael did not receive his final payment for it until 1514), with the help of Giulio Romano in the group on the right and of Giovanni da Udine in the group of women on the left. Among the Pope's retinue, by the left-hand edge of the painting, is a papal dignitary holding a scroll with the words "Io Pietro Foliariis Cremonensis" (I Pietro Foliaro of Cremona): but it has recently been concluded that the inscription has been tampered with and that the figure is in fact a self-portrait of Raphael himself.

THE PASSIONATE FORNARINA

The original of the beautiful women Raphael painted in his Roman period was la Fornarina. Raphael surprised her while she was paddling in the river and, "since he was amazingly desirous of every kind of beauty, finding her beautiful above all things, he straightway became enamoured of her and fixed all his thoughts upon her, nor had he any peace until he had made her his". La Fornarina is present in spirit in all his works. During his last illness she was constantly at his bedside. In his will he left her a share of his fortune so she might "live an honest woman". When the funeral procession wound its way through the streets of Rome, la Fornarina escaped from the people who were guarding her and flung herself upon the coffin, and allowed herself to be drawn away only when she was told that the Pope was thinking of beatifying Raphael and that therefore there must be no more talk of his earthly affections. Heartbroken, she entered the congregation of St. Apollonia in Trastevere not long after Raphael's death, and spent the rest of her life there in austere meditation.

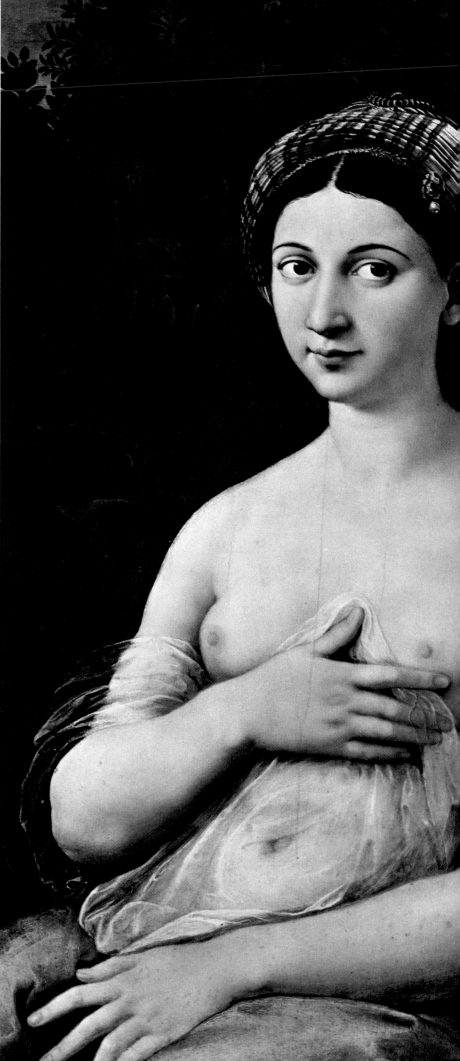

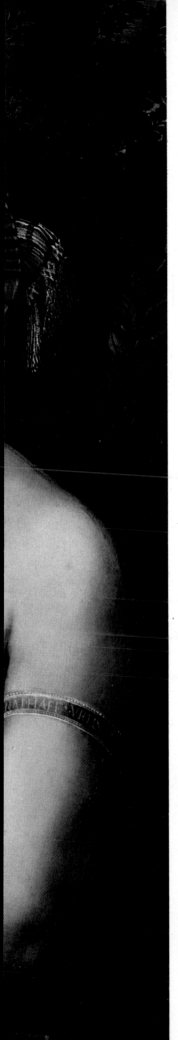

Here are the faces of those women who owe their beauty to la Fornarina. Extreme left: "La Velata", today in the Pitti. Centre: a portrait of la Fornarina herself, painted at the same time as the Vatican Stanze towards 1516. Below: four sacred figures with her features. The first, with eyes cast down, is the "Madonna di Foligno".

The next is the face of "St. Cecilia", of Bologna, who gazes heavenwards in ecstasy. Below left: the "Madonna della Seggiola", with her sweet and tranquil gaze, and beside her the beautiful Sistine "Madonna". Critics have reached agreement on the accuracy of these identifications after a great deal of controversy.

A FANTASTIC ZOO

Facing page: a detail from a flock of doves drawing the chariot of Venus in "The Story of Psyche" in the Farnesina. Immediately below: Attila's horse as it rears up in "The Meeting of Attila" in the Stanza di Eliodoro. (Compare the rearing horse shown here with that in the "St. George" which appears on page 9.) Below: the animals filing two by two in well-behaved decorum past Noah and his household in "Leaving the Ark", a fresco in the third bay of the Vatican Logge— the Logge were designed by Bramante and completed by Raphael, "more decoratively and harmoniously", according to Vasari, after the death of his illustrious predecessor.

Raphael portrayed all kinds of animals from doves to elephants: they make an unexpected zoo, glimpsed in the details of his pictures. In "The Story of Psyche", in the Farnesina, doves, eagles and griffins soar aloft, while down below we see a crocodile, a sea horse and a wolfhound. In "The Triumph of Galatea" there are fishes and dolphins. The fiery horses in the frescoes of the Vatican Stanze have a vigour far removed from the static quality of the horses of his Florentine period. In "The Story of Noah" lions, greyhounds and porcupines walk past two-by-two—as well as the mythical and symbolic unicorn, which also lays its head on the lap of the "Young Woman" in the Borghese Gallery. In the mouldings of the Vatican Logge and in a wood inlay in the Stanze della Segnatura there is even the portrait, after a design by Raphael, of a famous white elephant very popular with Leo X. Called Hanno, it had been brought to Rome by the Portuguese ambassador, where it had genuflected three times before the Pope and touched his sandal with its trunk. Hanno died of a heart attack in 1516.

CHARACTERS IN FLIGHT

If Leonardo was concerned with the mechanics of flight, Raphael was skilled at portraying it. Here are two examples. On the left, the figures of St. Peter and St. Paul, flying with unsheathed swords above the heads of the dignitaries in "The Meeting of Attila". (The background can be identified as ancient Rome, with a basilica, an aqueduct, the Colosseum, and the Meta Romuli.) Below, from "The Expulsion of Heliodorus", one of the avenging angels who is driving the sacrilegious criminal before him with a bunch of rods. His foot has only just touched the ground, and his garments are billowing out behind him as though he were still in flight.

HIS REPORTER'S EYE

After the celestial beings seen in flight, here we find mere mortals seized by Raphael's brush in a series of "snapshots" which capture the feeling and spontaneity of a passing moment. From "The Mass of Bolsena", for example, comes the detail reproduced below. Two bystanders close behind the celebrant gesture in amazement at the miracle they have just seen taking place, while the torches beneath the balcony flicker agitatedly. In the centre illustration, a man with tousled hair is climbing onto one of the temple pillars to witness more clearly the expulsion of Heliodorus, while someone else, with his clothes flying out behind him, is clutching him round the

waist. On the right, another person captured in the instant of moving, one of the little water-carriers in the "Incendio del Borgo" turns suddenly to call for fresh help. The subject of this fresco is taken from the Liber Pontificalis, *which tells how the terrible fire raging through the Roman suburb of Borgo in 847 was miraculously extinguished when* Leo IV gave his blessing from the Vatican Church. Raphael's skill at producing life-like paintings is confirmed by an anecdote which tells how one day the Papal Secretary, Baldassarre Turini, entering the room where Raphael's portrait of Leo X was hanging, took it to be the Pope himself and devoutly went to kneel before it.

RAPHAEL'S BIBLE

Below: some of the episodes which make up "The Bible of Raphael": they were painted with the help of his pupils, and, in particular, of Penni and Giulio Romano, and cannot be considered as being among his best work. Immediately below: "God Separates the Sun and the Moon", in which the figure of God flies above the as yet uninhabited earth. At the bottom: "God Creates the Animals"; here God walks through a fantastic world in which living creatures seem gradually to be taking shape. The animals were probably painted by Giovanni da Udine. On the opposite page, four other biblical scenes. Top

During the first months of 1519 the frescoes in the Vatican Logge were completed, and on June 11 the Treasury paid out "25 ducats to the artisans who have painted the Logge". Planned by Bramante and completed by Raphael, the Logge consist of 13 arches stretching for 70 yards. Behind each arch is a bay with four frescoes: the first 12 depict incidents from the Old Testament, the last shows one from the New. These 52 scenes make up the so-called "Bible of Raphael", and are among his last works. The scenes are for the most part richly framed by coloured and gilded plaster mouldings, with decorations and grotesques at the corners inspired by the Domus Aurea which had just been discovered. In making the mouldings Raphael employed the work of Giovanni da Udine, who used the classical mixture of chalk and powdered marble, and of Pierin del Vaga, whose amalgam had a finer finish. One of these mouldings shows what is probably Raphael's workshop. At that time the artist was living like a prince: he owned a magnificent palace in Borgo Nuovo, designed by Bramante and bought from the Caprivi for 3,600 ducats; and he lived surrounded by works of art and protected by a guard of servants who kept at bay a succession of importuning people. Even the Duke of Ferrara's ambassador, who kept calling to ask for "The Triumph of Bacchus", was shown the door by Raphael's servants, and had to follow the painter through the streets of Rome before he could talk to him. The artist was also preoccupied with the preservation of Roman antiquities as entrusted him by the Pope, and often requisitioned the finest items brought to light in the excavations to enrich the papal collection. From a sworn statement dated 1518 we learn that one of the Capitoline keepers, who had inherited as his private property several antique statues, came up against Raphael, who wanted to take them over for the papal collection. He was also in charge of all the cultural enterprises ordered by the Pope; when Ariosto's play "I Suppostiti" was performed in 1518 in the Castel San Angelo, Raphael was appointed to design and paint the sets. Since all the famous people of his time were imploring him to paint their portraits, the painter was forced to organize his work as a "team effort", having parts of it carried out by apprentices.

left: "God Creates Eve", and entrusts her to Adam, who has only just awoken; at his feet crouches a rabbit, a symbol of fertility. Top right: "Isaac and Rebecca Watched by Abimilech"— a particularly harmonious and balanced composition in which there is more evidence of the hand of Raphael himself. Below

left: "Joseph Explains Pharaoh's Dreams", in which Joseph faces an astonished court. In the two tondi in the background above the windows are depicted the seven years of plenty and the seven years of famine, symbolized by the ears of wheat and the cattle. Finally, below right: "Moses

Makes the Waters Gush from the Living Rock", a moment during Moses' return to the Promised Land. The Logge frescoes, exposed to the elements for centuries and glassed over only in the 1850s, have suffered serious damage and been retouched over and over again.

69

TAPESTRIES OF SILK AND GOLD

Goethe considered that Raphael's tapestries were his only works which seemed anything more than mediocre when compared to the roof of the Sistine Chapel by Michelangelo. Ordered by Leo X to cover the walls of the Sistine Chapel, they had indeed to face a supreme challenge, but even on this occasion Raphael met it with genius. It was customary at that time for the lower part of the walls to be covered on solemn occasions by seven great tapestries showing the principal stages of the Passion; these had become so worn with age that Pope Leo X charged Raphael to design ten more, which would illustrate the origins of the Church and its first encounters with the pagan world. Raphael's total payment amounted to upwards of 1,000 scudi. His cartoons were real paintings, in size pigment on paper, and of immense dimensions— 17 ft high × 16–20 ft wide. They were inspired by the Acts of the Apostles. These are the themes: "The Miraculous Draught of Fishes", "The Curing of the Cripple", "The Stoning of St. Stephen", "The Conversion of St. Paul", "The Blinding of Elymas", "The Sacrifice of Lystra", "The Death of Ananias", "St. Paul in Prison", and "The Sermon of St. Paul". The cartoons were sent to Brussels to the famous weaver Pieter Van Aelst (where Dürer also saw them) and were carried out mainly in silk and gold. The first seven tapestries to arrive in Rome were shown in the Sistine Chapel for the Christmas of 1519, and aroused both praise and criticism: Sebastiano del Piombo, for example, found them too crude in colour. They cost the Pope 1,600 gold ducats each. Three of the cartoons have been lost; seven were bought by Rubens in 1630 from the heirs of Van Aelst and sent to Charles I of England for his workshops. Then, on the death of the King, Cromwell bought them all for £300, and today they are in the Victoria and Albert Museum. The tapestries underwent a series of mishaps before coming to rest in the Vatican. On the death of Leo X they were pawned for 5,000 ducats: then in 1527, during the sack of Rome, they were sold by the mercenaries to merchants who burned part of them in order to extract the gold from the weaving, and resold the remainder. They were finally recovered and returned to the Vatican in 1808, where they are still to be seen.

"The Miraculous Draught of Fishes" illustrates the passage from St. Luke, "Fear not, for henceforward ye shall be fishers of men". There exist several variants of this tapestry, considered one of the finest of the series. The second, entitled "The Sacrifice of Lystra", tells how, after St. Paul and Barnabas had cured a life-long cripple, the crowd thought the two saints were gods from Olympus and wished to sacrifice to them, but the two Christians refused. Opposite, left: the Greeks with their sacrificial offering.

HIS UNFINISHED
MASTERPIECE

In 1517 Giulio de' Medici ordered two pictures: one from Sebastiano del Piombo, "The Raising of Lazarus", and one from Raphael, "The Transfiguration". He wished to arouse the spirit of rivalry between the two artists. Sebastiano, one of Michelangelo's friends and therefore antagonistic towards Raphael, set himself to work at a feverish pace and towards Christmas, two years later, finished his painting. Raphael on the other hand made no attempt to hurry, and though in the later months, as Vasari said, "his hand was ever at work", he managed to finish only the top part of the painting before he was struck down by the fever to which he finally succumbed only weeks later. (Sebastiano was eaten up by envy: he even spread the rumour that Raphael was using as a model a celebrated courtesan called Imperia. Raphael's death silenced his spiteful tongue.) Vasari attributed Raphael's early death to amorous excesses, and many others openly accused la Fornarina. According to another version, however, Raphael brought upon himself a "continuous and acute" fever by reaching the Vatican much overheated and then being kept for a long time with Leo X "in rooms so cold and draughty that the sweat chilled him to the bone". The doctors diagnosed pleurisy, and, as was then customary, subjected him to a blood-letting which succeeded in killing him. Feeling himself close to death, Raphael made a sensible division of his fortune, which amounted to 16,000 ducats. The land he had bought as a site for a new palace was divided between an uncle and a friend who was a goldsmith. He left 1,000 ducats for the maintenance of the chapel in the Pantheon in which he wished to be buried. Every servant had 300 scudi, and la Fornarina was bequeathed enough for her to live decently. His school and workshop were left to Giulio Romano and Penni: everything else went to his relatives in Urbino. "Confessed and penitent", after having sent la Fornarina from his rooms, Raphael died on the evening of April 6, 1520, on Good Friday, on the same day and at the same hour on which he had been born. Shortly before his death a portico in the papal palace threatened to collapse, and immediately afterwards a ceiling fell down in the Vatican: it seemed as though Rome itself was in mourning.

72

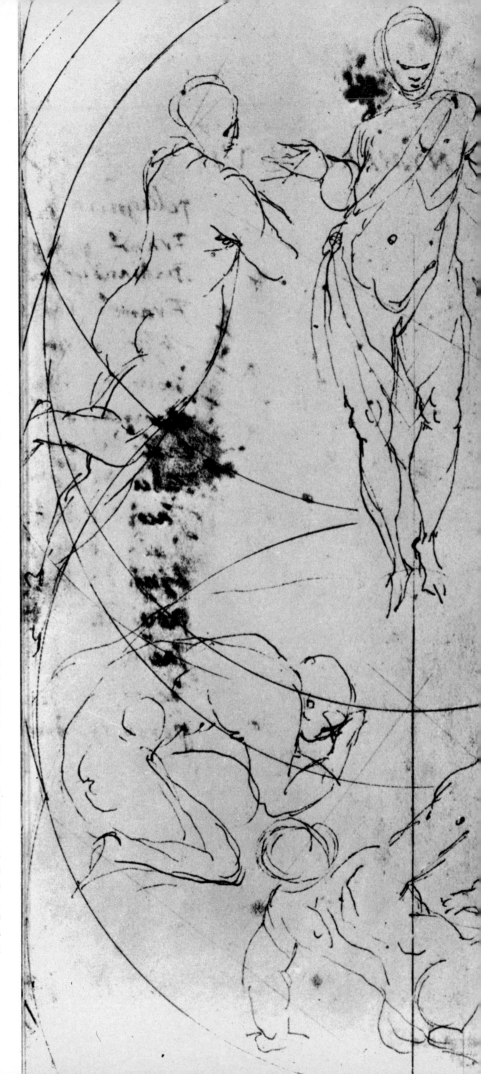

Left: in a framework of circles, the preliminary sketches for "The Transfiguration". Raphael succeeded in finishing only the upper part of this painting, with the figure of Christ; in the lower part the group of the nine apostles on the left was almost finished, but the epileptic boy on the right was barely drawn in outline. The work was finished by Giulio Romano and Francesco Penni, to whom, rather than to a "caprice" of Raphael's, should be attributed the use of "printer's smoke-black" which later caused the colours to darken. The canvas, placed in San Pietro di Montorio in Rome, was later looted by the French, and restored to the Vatican in 1815.

Cleaned + restored: 1978

The head of the transfigured Christ: Raphael's last and unfinished work is a revelation of the highest expression of his art. His pupils hung his "Transfiguration" over the head of the dying painter's bed, "in such a way that each one who gazed thereon and witnessed thus the dead body and the painting which seemed to live and breathe felt his heart like to break from grief". Raphael was given an ornate funeral worthy of a prince of the Church, and mourned by the whole of Rome. He was buried in the Pantheon beside the little mamola bella, his betrothed, Maria Bibbiena, who had died only a few months before him, at the age of 18.

Few artists have enjoyed during their lifetime so universal a recognition as Raphael. If his rivalry with Michelangelo had not aroused in many an almost reverential fear, he would have reigned in Rome with even greater honours. His painting was "classical" in the precise sense of the word. It expresses that ideal of beauty characteristic of the Renaissance, derived from serenity, natural perfection, and the joy of living. Indeed Raphael himself embodies the ideal of the Renaissance artist. He succeeded in establishing himself as a great master in all forms of art, from oil painting to frescoes, and in all kinds of design, from flower drawings to anatomical studies: from cartoons for tapestries to archaeology and architecture. He also tried his hand at poetry: there exist five sonnets which express his burning passion for his loved one. Raphael attained to a marvellous kind of equanimity: he was "never overwrought, never mean, never trivial", as Delacroix commented. After his death, however, his followers obscured the true sense of his glory. Where he had been truly "classical" they became merely "academic". New aesthetic ideals replaced those of the Renaissance, and from the Baroque age onwards Raphael was reproached precisely for that noble and harmonious "grace" which had been the hall-mark of his art.

1483—April 6; born in Urbino; his parents were the painter Giovanni Santi di Pietro and Magia di Battista di Nicola Ciarla.
1491—October 7: death of his mother.
1494—August 1: death of his father and first teacher, Giovanni Santi.
1495—He leaves probably for Perugia and begins working with Perugino.
1500—December 10: with Evangelista di Pian di Meleto he receives the commission for the Pala del Beato Nicola da Tolentino for the Church of Sant'Agostino in Città di Castello. Between 1500 and 1503 can also be dated "The Resurrection" now in the Art Museum of São Paulo in Brazil, and certain other works, among them the Mond "Crucifixion", now in the National Gallery, London, and the "Incoronazione", now in the Vatican.
1504—"The Betrothal of the Virgin", now in the Brera Gallery in Milan.
1505—He finishes the fresco of "The Holy Trinity and Saints" in the Church of San Severo in Perugia (thought by some critics to be later). From 1503-6 he finishes the "Pala Colonna", now in the Metropolitan Museum in New York, and the "Pala Ansidei", now in the National Gallery, London.
1507—"The Deposition", now in the Borghese Gallery in Rome.
1508—A year spent between Rome and Florence, probably the date of the "Cowper Madonna" now in the National Gallery of Art in Washington.
1509—Now permanently in Rome, on October 4 he is nominated Writer of the Papal Briefs. According to a document dated January 13, he must also have started this year on the work in the Vatican Stanze.
1511—This is the date chalked on the frescoes of "Parnassus" and "The Virtues" in the Stanza della Segnatura in the Vatican.
1512—Date given beneath the fresco of "The Mass of Bolsena" in the Stanza di Eliodoro. It was probably during this time that he started work in the apartments of Julius II, as mentioned in a letter from Grossino to Isabella d'Este.
1513—He receives 50 ducats from Leo X's treasury to start work again on the frescoes in the Vatican Stanze.
1514—The frescoes in the Stanza di Eliodoro date from this year. He paints the fresco of "The Sibyls" in the Church of Santa Maria della Pace in Rome, is nominated architect of St. Peter's on April 1 and receives the commission for "St. Cecilia", now in the Bologna Gallery.
1515—On August 27 is nominated Custodian of Roman Antiquities; in November he leaves Rome and, as Bandinelli recalls, goes to Florence to join a conference of all the leading Italian architects to discuss the plans for the façade of San Lorenzo.
1516—He starts work on the fresco of the "Incendio del Borgo" in the Stanza called after it. This is also the date shown on the mosaics of Santa Maria del Popolo in Rome, completed from designs by Raphael. In a letter dated April 19, 1516, Bembo mentions several portraits by Raphael, amongst them that of "Baldassare Castiglione". In December he is paid the fee for the cartoons of the Vatican tapestries, which must therefore have been completed some time before this date.
1517—In a letter from the ambassador Constabili to the Duke of Ferrara he mentions that the pictures in the Stanza dell'Incendio del Borgo in the Vatican have been completed, and indeed beneath the "Giuramento di Leone X" appears the date MCCCCCXVII. He also mentions in the same letter "The Triumph of Bacchus" which Raphael was to paint for the Duke of Ferrara. In September of this year he continues to work on "The Transfiguration", now in the Vatican Gallery, which he started in January. In November he sends to the Duke of Ferrara the cartoon for "The Battle of Ostia", a fresco from the Stanza dell'Incendio del Borgo. Towards the end of this year he also finishes the fresco of "Psyche" in the Loggia of the Farnesina, as is mentioned by Leonardo Sellaio to Michelangelo on the following January 1.
1518—To this year can be dated the portrait of Lorenzo de' Medici. Leo X nominated Raphael and Antonio da Sangallo the Younger, Masters of the Roads, that is, town-planners of the city of Rome.
1519—According to a letter dated June 16 from Baldassare Castiglione to Isabella d'Este, the work on the Logge frescoes—called "The Bible of Raphael"—was just completed. Certainly from this year can be dated studies in preparation for a map of ancient Rome. During the Christmas celebrations seven tapestries from Raphael's series are shown in the Sistine Chapel.
1520—On April 6 he dies in Rome aged only 37. He leaves several works unfinished which will later be completed by his followers.

The works reproduced in this volume belong to the following collections: Rome: Farnesina, pp. 42, 43, 62. Bologna: Picture Gallery, p. 39. Urbino: Duke's Palace, pp. 4, 5, 6, 37. Milan: Brera Gallery, pp. 10, 11. Florence: Uffizi, pp. 7, 12, 13, 23, 24, 27, 30, 32, 34, 38, 39. Siena Cathedral, p. 7. London: National Gallery, p. 8. Chantilly Museum, pp. 8, 20. Paris: Louvre, pp. 9, 15, 22, 24, 30–31, 36. Caen Museum, p. 10. Florence: Pitti Palace, Palatina Gallery, pp. 14, 19, 30, 33, 37, 60. Vienna: Kunsthistorisches Museum, p. 15. Munich: Picture Gallery, p. 25. Berlin: Kaiser Friedrich Museum, pp. 20–21. Rome: St. Peter's, p. 26. Rome: Borghese Gallery, pp. 27, 60. Vatican Picture Gallery, pp. 21, 35, 73, 74. New York: Metropolitan Museum, p. 31. Baltimore Museum, p. 32. Madrid: Prado, p. 33. Dresden: Museum, pp. 41, 42–43. Vatican Museum, pp. 44, 45, 46–47, 48–49, 50–51, 52, 53, 54, 55, 56, 57, 58, 59, 63, 64, 65, 66, 67. Vatican Logge, pp. 63, 68, 69. Vatican: Arazzi Gallery, pp. 70, 71. Oxford: Ashmolean Museum, pp. 24, 28, 29. Photographic references: Ghilardi, pp. 21, 26–27, 35, 42, 43, 45, 46–47, 59, 60, 62, 65, 66, 70–71, 74. Tourist Bureau, Urbino, pp. 4–5, 6, 37. Marzari, pp. 5, 21. Ronchini, p. 5. Caramelli, p. 7. Fleming, p. 8. Arborio Mella, pp. 8, 20. Giraudon, pp. 9, 10. Scarnati, pp. 9, 15, 22, 24, 36. Alinari, pp. 10, 24, 28, 29, 30, 47, 54, 71. Scala, pp. 11, 12, 13, 14, 23, 33, 34, 38, 39, 60, 61, 67, 73. Meyer, p. 15. Blauel, pp. 18, 25, 35, 40, 41, 61. Mori, pp. 26, 27. Bevilacqua, pp. 30–31. Mercurio, pp. 30, 37, 60. Gardner Collection, p. 33. Del Priore, pp. 44, 54–55. Studium, pp. 48–49, 50–51, 52, 53, 56, 57, 58, 63, 64, 66, 68, 69; and the Mondadori Photographic Archives.